An Introduction to Indu

An Introduction to Indu

MW00946385

About the Author

Scott Mackay was born in Detroit in 1952, moved to New England at 5 years old, and moved to Georgia in 1979. At an early age he was curious about how things worked and was always tinkering with things and experimenting with improvements. If something broke, he would try to redesign it so it could never break that way again. He was soon the go to person in the family for fixing all things broken.

Besides good fix-it skills, he had good imagination and analytic abilities and could use those abilities to figure out how something was intended to work along with how it might be changed or used in a different way to become something even better and more useful.

He also had a good knack for determining the best level of abstraction to describe a process problem. This is an ability that many people struggle with, especially those who can't leave out irrelevant details to shorten a process description into a crisp, clear, and understandable form.

Working life started right out of high school and college was relegated to nights and weekends. His interest in industrial engineering came naturally as everything he worked on was a personal challenge to determine the one best way to perform the work.

Over the 50+ years of his career there was always a demand for his skills and the paychecks were ample enough to afford raising a family, taking nice vacations, and putting away for a comfortable retirement.

An Introduction to Industrial Engineering

Dedication

I would like to thank my family, the many teachers and professors
from my college days, and the many fellow industrial engineers who
mentored me over the years to help me be my best.

About This Book

Industrial Engineering is an exciting field that sometimes seems to
be hidden in the background. The goal of writing this book is to give
the reader enough information to assess if this might be the right
career for them.

This book is intended to give the reader a look at some of the many
facets of the industrial engineering field. It is deliberately short,
gives a glimpse of the day-to-day activities that might be
encountered, and includes some personal stories to illustrate the
details involved. The intention is to be educational without being
tutorial while providing a somewhat comprehensive overview to
help the reader decide if industrial engineering might be the right
career for them.

An Introduction to Industrial Engineering

Table of Contents

An Introduction to Industrial Engineering

Introduction

Most people are familiar with the engineering disciplines of Mechanical, Electrical, Computer Science and such. Industrial Engineering is focused on how we do work. Work? Yes, from things like doing house chores, making a meal, painting a room, to assembling an automobile, processing bank statements, and building rocket ships.

The Industrial Engineer is focused on determining the most efficient way to get the work performed. This efficiency is measured in total activity time and total cycle time (aka tact time). Cycle time is the time to complete a workflow from start to finish. Cycle time translates to time from getting a work order, to perform some work, to delivering the finished work to a customer. The faster it can happen, the better advantage you have on your competitor.

Total activity time is the time needed to perform all the activities needed for the product being delivered. It differs from total cycle time by the fact that activities done in parallel will shorten the total cycle time while total activity time might remain constant. The shorter the activity time, the less effort will be needed to deliver the product or service.

Maybe not under its contemporary name, Industrial Engineering has been around since before the building of the great pyramids. Most people want efficiency in work and people will instinctively try new approaches and refine the work process until it worked well and had little waste efforts involved. For this author, it has been an ever-exciting career that always kept me busy and paid the bills nicely.

Is Industrial Engineering the right career for you? God gives us each special talents and tapping into these talents will almost certainly help make whatever career you choose seem more like fun and challenging than a career that yields you only drudgery and obligation. Are you the kind of person who is quick to point out better ways to do things? Do you find yourself thinking out the steps to do work and sorting out unnecessary actions, combining actions where possible, and defining the easiest way to get the work accomplished? Are you creative and able to invent new solutions? If yes, this might be the right career for you. You might start as an Industrial Engineer and grow to be an Industrial Scientist, Software Business Analyst, Producibility Engineer, Workplace Safety Engineer, Project Estimator, Robotics Engineer (yes, robots do work which puts them in the Industrial Engineering domain), Artificial Intelligence Engineer, etc.

Industrial Engineering is about all work and anything that influences that work. If something affects how work can be performed, the Industrial Engineering is interested in it. Things that can affect how work is performed includes the many ancillary disciplines such as Quality Engineering, Production Engineering, Workstation & Plant Layout Design, Logistics, Traffic Flow Engineering, etc.

When it comes to choosing a career, you should be looking for something you will be good at and enjoy doing. Having fun at your job is a good sign that you have the right career. If you must force yourself to show up to work each day, you are probably in the wrong job.

The flowchart

The flowchart is the primary tool for studying work. It lets you document how work is performing currently and how work might be after your improvements. And it helps to communicate the details to others.

Flowcharts are one of those things that tend to fill quickly with details and grow to exceed what can be viewed and comprehended at one time. To accommodate this, we design flowcharts with a hierarchy. This means that what might be a single activity on one page can viewed in deeper detail by "drilling down" to the next level of abstraction to see the lower-level activities that occur.

An Introduction to Industrial Engineering

Being good at visualization of each level of abstraction is helpful. A common convention is to define each level by a number, with level zero being the top.

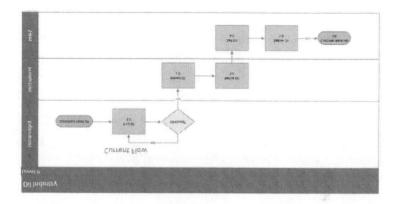

An example of a level zero workflow for the oil industry would be: Find Oil, Extract Oil, Refine Oil, Sell Oil, Deliver Oil. Levels below each of these activities could be level 2, by department, level 3, by work team. Level 4, by workstation, and level 5, by action performed. Note that activity names always start with an action verb and include the noun object being worked on. This convention helps describe the work activity in the fewest words.

Flowcharts are made up by a simple set of symbols:

1) The trigger. This symbol indicates the start of the workflow and should state what event has occurred to trigger this start. Example: Need Oil for Sales.
2) The conclusion. This symbol indicates the end of the workflow and should state what event has occurred to signal completion of the workflow. Example: Oil is delivered to customer.
3) The work activity. This symbol states the activity being performed. Example: Extract Oil
4) The decision gate. This symbol is used when a conditional situation exists that must be satisfied before moving to the next activity. Example: Oil Found?

7

An Introduction to Industrial Engineering
5) The Swim Lane. Swim lanes allow grouping activities within the department, team, workstation being depicted in the flowchart.

This simple set of symbols is all that is needed. You want your work to be easily understood by your audience. There are other more complex sets of workflow symbols out there, but they generally are too complicated to be understood by the lay person. Your work is worthless if your audience cannot understand it.

A common addition to a workflow is to number the activities to aid in tracing to lower-level workflows. For example, "Find Oil" might be numbered 1.0 at level zero. At level two, each activity for Find Oil would be numbered "1.1", '1.2", etc. At level three each activity for "1.1" would be numbered "1.1.1", "1.1.2" etc. When my workflows get complex, this is my go-to solution.

Level 5 is one that is a bit different that the other levels. It focuses on work at the physical level such as reaching for a part, transporting a part, positioning a part, releasing a part, etc. Flowcharting at this level of detail becomes necessary when studying the actual human or machine movements to perform work at a workstation.

Many years ago, Frank and Lillian Gilbreth studied human work actions and defined a set of symbols they named "Therbligs" (Gilbreth spelled backwards) for documenting human/machine level work activities. I recommend looking them up to see their pioneering contributions to industrial engineering.

The process of creating flowcharts can be done many ways. I will often start by some interviews with experts and start drafting the big picture. Note that I am not trying to document the whole universe, only the work area of interest to the area I want to improve. Trying to document the whole would be wasteful and with continuous change in our modern world, the work would be obsolete in a short time anyways. After getting the big picture, I like to see the actual work being performed and document it more accurately by observation and interviews with the people performing the work.

It is important to use clear names for each activity in your workflow. Your audience needs to see and interpret the same picture you are creating. Also stay on the same level of abstraction. I have occasionally found myself stymied in my workflow creation only to realize I had two levels of abstraction in play. Also, names should use business language. Never use technical language, you are analyzing the business workflow, not the technical workflow. Your workflow isn't worth a hill of beans if your team can't understand it.

While observing the work, it is also useful to collect data such as how long each activity takes. This data will be useful in tracking the time saved if a better process is developed. My go to approach for timing a task is to ask if I can video what they are doing. Most people don't like to be timed but being video seems to be ok. Once I have the video, I can make my own determination of what time I think the activity should take and then factor in some time for everyday variability.

There is occasionally the need to develop a flowchart for work that has not yet been performed. For example, maybe a new product or service is being contemplated. In this case your ability to visualize the future work activities comes into play. You might not get it perfect, but you should be able to get close.

Also, the subject of estimating the amount of work in labor hours and flowtime might come up. In this case, experience helps greatly along with the ability to find similar work activities with known work times to use for comparison. Knowing the estimated time with help with planning the workforce needs and assuring the new activities are cost feasible.

During the American Industrial Revolution, a man named Frederick Taylor, also thought of as the father of modern industrial

An Introduction to Industrial Engineering

engineering, studied brick masons working on new factories being built. He determined the best workflow for laying bricks and set a time standard for how many bricks a good mason should be able to set. This time standard was used to set fair pay rates and an incentive pay if a mason exceeded the standard. The changes he made created moderate improvement to the speed of building these massive brick factories. I recommended looking this man up and learning more about his contributions to America.

As an industrial engineer, you should be able to create flowcharts rapidly and in the middle of a room of people if needed. In a group setting I will often be projecting my laptop PC screen so others in the room can see my work and contribute to it as I draft it out. I will typically ignore neatness and collect the workflow data during the meeting. Later I will go back and neaten it all up to a professional level.

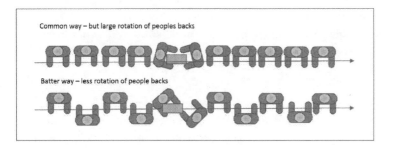

As an example of level 5, physical movements in the workflow, let me use an use a scenario I come across quite often in my volunteer life, the "Bucket Brigade". We use bucket brigades to move objects from point A to point B in a rapid process. Typically, you will find a long line of people all facing say north aligned in a say east to west line. Each person will rotate 85 degrees left to grab an object and then rotates 170 degrees right to hand the object off to the next person in line. This repeats while each time the person is being careful to get eye contact on the object, make sure that have it in hand, and doing the same as they release it to the next person. This is a less safe way to work. Fatigue and back pain are certain to set in quickly. The modification needed is to have every other person in the north facing line to turn around and face south. This simple change reduces the rotation of the body during object exchange by better than half. Each person will now rotate 40 degrees left/right to grab the object being passed and then rotates only 80 degrees to hand the object off. Eye contact with the objects is also improved.

Most of my workflows are kept simple and suitable for viewing on a single computer screen without much scrolling to see it all. But occasionally I will create a larger printout workflow in poster size or wall mural size that would be impractical for use in a conference room projector screen. This larger format is generally used to share the workflow with the whole company so everyone can follow what we are changing.

Quality of your work is also extremely important. Take time to check you details and assure every step of interest has been included. Being a dyslectic since birth, I have a built-in reflex to check my work and follow the details. I believe this has worked to my advantage. Another technique I like to deliberately use is to set my work aside, do something else for a while, and come back later to take a fresh look and do my proof reading.

Reverse Engineering

In order to decompose a workflow down to its roots to perform analysis on it you will often need to reverse engineer the activities that have been previously automated. Proper analysis of a workflow requires all of the business activities be defined. Once all has been exposed, decisions on combining, eliminating, and simplification can be made. Reverse engineering often requires imagination and critical thinking to fill in the blanks that the automation is performing. This can be a daunting task but understanding the goal of the workflow usually helps reveal what activities would logically be occurring.

Why is this so important? I have lost track at how many times I discovered that obsolete, redundant, or incorrect activities were

An Introduction to Industrial Engineering
hidden in the automation. Automations added at one time to improve the workflow were now working against it. In one case I discovered software was being utilized and supported that was no longer needed. Documenting the real workflow revealed it and allowed the situation to be corrected.

Bottlenecks

Capacity Analysis

When it comes to workflows, especially in factories, there are typically inherent flow choke points called "bottlenecks". This is a point where the flow of work is restricted by the capacity of the tools or people performing the work. For example, a tool that installs a certain rivet might only have the capacity to do it 100 times per hour. If more than 100 are needed, a second tool will need to be purchased. When studying a workflow, the Industrial Engineer should be identifying the bottlenecks and noting the workflow rate where they will impact the process. Note that any scheduled downtime such as Preventative Maintenance (PM) must also be accounted for. This helps with planning to future rate increases and is one of the many value-added things an industrial engineering does.

Capacity bottlenecks can raise havoc in a "push approach" to production control. Since work queues are not controlled, it is easy to have days were the capacity of your bottleneck workstation(s) will temporarily constrain the production velocity.

If a "pull approach" were in use, it would not be possible to exceed the capacity of the bottleneck workstation. I go into deeper detail on the differences between a "push approach" and a "pull approach" in a later chapter.

Break Fix

It seems most things we buy these days are designed for a set lifetime. In industry it is the same. Equipment is most often designed for self-obsolescence and spare part sales. A philosophy of making machines that "can work" trumps over machines that "can't fail". As industrial engineers we can identify the failure points of equipment and work with other engineers to redesign for a can't fail solution. In my own observation, I have seen companies buy the best of the best equipment and then send it straight to their own machine shop to be retrofitted up to meet the rigor standards they need for safety and reliability when the equipment is put to use. Awkward, but reality. Broken equipment stops production and costs money. Also, storing spare parts also costs money. Redesigning equipment to minimize the amount of spare parts needed is usually a cost beneficial move. The cost trade analysis to eliminate failure points is usually an easy one.

Out in the real world, many companies take redesigning of equipment to prevent downtime as a mandatory fact of life. Other less enlightened companies simply accept that equipment fails, and you fix it. Can you guess who has the more efficient approach. As Industrial Engineers we often find ourselves teaching industry leaders the best practices. Of course, we can only lead them to the better solutions, they still need to take the steps to adopt them.

Years ago, I was working in the mining industry and we had these giant ore boring machines that would occasionally burn out a set of expensive drive belts when something clogged the boring teeth. Downtime was several hours, and the belts were expensive. To make it worse, the foreman would blame the equipment operator for being too hard on the machine. I sketched out the drive belt situation and met with the machine shop mechanical engineers to brainstorm better solutions. They came up with replacing the belts

An Introduction to Industrial Engineering
with a sprocket driven chain and added a slip clutch to release automatically if the drive pressure exceeded a certain point. This solution would stop the drive action when the boring teeth became clogged and gave the equipment operator the opportunity to reverse the drive and unclog the teeth. After retrofitting the machines, they never had to fix the drives again and no more expensive drive belts wherever purchased. I use this story to help drive home the point of taking charge of your equipment and eliminating downtime.

Brainstorming

When looking for better solutions, I often will call for a brainstorming session. It never ceases to amaze me how effective a brainstorming session can be at finding solutions to problems. To prepare, I write a clear description of the problem and invite people close to the problem to participate. I like a group size of 7 to 10 so we have enough but not too many. Brainstorming has only a few rules:

1) No one is to criticize other people's suggestions
2) Everyone should make suggestions
3) No suggestion is considered unacceptable, even if is not really feasible.

We go around the room with each person submitting a suggestion on their turn. My role as facilitator is to record each suggestion where everyone can see them. We continue around the room again and again until everyone says there are no more suggestions. Note that occasionally I might throw in a suggestion too.

Next step is to rank the list by most feasible to least. This brings the best suggestions to the top of the list. Then there is a discussion and vote on which suggestion we should pursue. It is like magic, at the start of the session we have a problem to be solved, about an hour later we have a solution that is supported by the team. Doesn't get better than that.

An Introduction to Industrial Engineering
I find myself facilitating brainstorming sessions quite often. Usually, it is at the start of a project or when a problem is discovered in a workflow that I am analyzing.

Sometimes I will use a brainstorming session to conduct a root cause analysis where we are trying to determine possible reasons causing a process defect. All the possible causes can get recorded onto an Ishakawa Chart to document the big picture. Eventually we can zoom in on the most probable causes and develop solutions to eliminate them from causing any negative impacts.

There is a thing called synergism, the sum of the team output is greater than the total inputs. Brainstorming proves this concept. Sure, I could probably come up with a solution myself, but it is so much better when the team invents the solution and stands behind it.

The Context Diagram

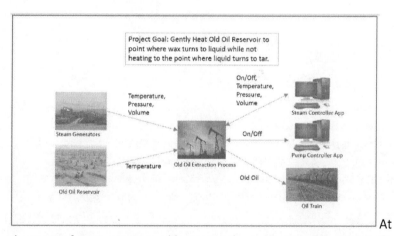

At the start of every project, I like to get the team together and craft a clear and precise statement of the business problem we are trying to solve. This puts us all on the same page with the same understanding of our goal.

An Introduction to Industrial Engineering
After some analysis work, I will next create a context diagram of the problem statement area within the business. With the business problem area of interest in the center, I add all the needed business information inputs to the left and outputs to the right. This creates a one-page pictorial view of the business problem domain. I also include the problem statement in this diagram. Think of it as an executive overview of the project goal.

Use Case Diagram

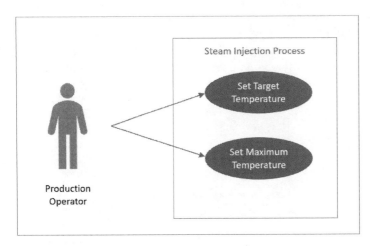

To further support the project, a comprehensive set of use case diagrams is helpful to have. A level zero diagram might include the use case feature sets. And a level 2 diagram might be created to show each use case within a feature set. Note that use cases typically show up as activities in your level 4 workflows. These diagrams might also be marked up to indicate existing, new, and changed use cases to give a sense of the planned workload for the project.

State Diagram

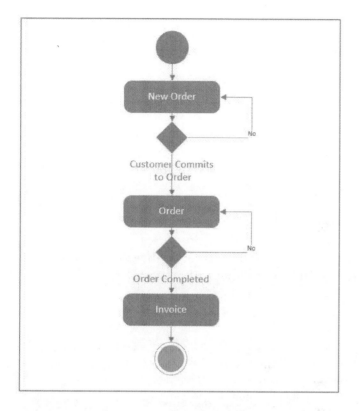

Some business objects change state over time and a state diagram is the best way to document this. For example, a Sales Order might start as a new order, change to an order in process, and then a completed order. The state diagram will document the name for each of these states and the event that triggered the event change. Having this diagram will reduce confusion in the team by keeping everyone on the same page.

Push versus Pull

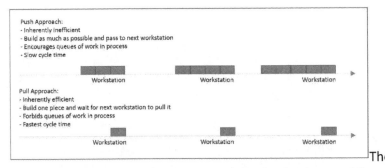

There are two popular approaches to managing a production workflow, push or pull. Push is inherently very inefficient, and Pull is inherently very efficient. You can guess which is the best practice. However, my personal observation is that for some reason people tend to gravitate to using a push approach. Maybe it's an education thing but I see it far too often in industry. We can thank Japan for perfecting the pull approach. They have a system called Kan-Ban which I encourage you to research and understand.

A push approach has production products being pushed toward completion along the workflow. When one activity is completed, the product is pushed into queue for the next operation. Push approaches are easily identified by the queues of product at each workstation. A larger than needed amount of product is in work at the same time and most of it is sitting awaiting work to be performed on it.

In a pull approach, a product is not moved to the next activity until that next activity has completed and signaled a readiness to start the next piece. In practice no product is queued, and each workstation focuses on one piece at a time. If the upstream station is not ready for their piece, they stop and wait. Once the piece moves on, they turn to the downstream workstation to pull their next piece to work on. At best the maximum number of pieces in work will be one per workstation. Having fewer pieces in work also

An Introduction to Industrial Engineering
minimizes the chances of damage to product, saves space, and
lowers risk of rework.

Part of achieving a good pull approach is line balancing. This is
where the correct amount of work has been allocated to each
workstation such that just of one workstation finishes their work,
the next workstation is just getting ready to pull it forward and do
their work.

A best practice I add to the pull approach is to empower the
workstation operators to help each other out in keeping the flow
running. I teach them that if the upstream pieces is still in work
when they complete their piece, ask them if they need help and
move over to help if needed. Same goes for when they are ready to
pull from the downstream workstation and that piece is not ready.
Teamwork can go a long way to smoothing out delays in the
process.

When I worked in the defense industry, I was asked to take on a
project that had been stalled and was failing. Some 1200 smart
bombs needed to be retrofitted with two resistors on a circuit
board in their autopilot. When I arrived on the site, I found a push
approach in place and lots of product in queue, so much that
moving around facility was difficult. After some analysis I
determined that 30 unique workstations were needed and
immediately laid out the floor space to build a serpentine of
workstations where pieces could be handed from one workstation
to another. I then marked out squares in bright tape on each
workstation to indicate where to place a part to be worked on and
where to place a part that was ready to move to the next
workstation. I had one exception area where I created a queue for
product that failed testing. I allowed 10 pieces maximum to be
staged here. This was one day's work for the troubleshooting
technician. If that queue got full, we stopped work and focused on
just it.

I implemented these taped signal squares over the weekend and called a meeting first thing on Monday to explain to the workforce how it would all work. It took a few days to clear out the queue of parts left from the push approach, but we soon had a steady and predictable flow of 6 autopilots retrofitted per day. This made forecasting my project completion date quite easy. Space cleared up in the factory and the operation became of interest to top managers as they brought in visitors to see what had been done. Even the customer was impressed. For me, it was straight forward industrial engineering work using a known best practice.

On a side note, that team asked me if they could have a signal for when each smart bomb was completed and heading to the warehouse. They wanted to make sure they were keeping up with their 6 pieces per day. I agreed and they decided to play Queen's "Another one bites the dust" over the plant public address system. For the next few months, we heard the song play its 6 times per day until we completed the project. Who says industrial engineering can't be fun.

Change Overs

Change overs are another area of interest to the Industrial Engineer. This is the situation that occurs when a workstation needs to be switched from building one product to building another product. Ideally, the workstation is designed to support all products all the time such that there is no impact due to a change over. But reality is that often work is needed to make the conversion. The industrial engineer needs to determine a solution for a minimal amount of downtime in making the change over. This is often accomplished by have new stock and tools on a mobile platform that can be wheeled into position in seconds. In some cases, it's more difficult but at the end of the day the important thing is to make the change over go quickly and get production up a running. Again, going for the shortest cycle time and shortest total activity time.

Batches

Batching is another area that has inherent inefficiency. Batching is when we plan a set of pieces to be built and staged to support production. The batch size might be determined by an economical breakpoint based on change over times. Batching is common when a push approach is being used. The problem with batching is you are building product ahead of when it will be needed. It now has to be stored, protected from damage, and tracked to be sure it gets used when needed. In the pull approach, these parts would not be touched until a sales order is in place and the product is being built to support that order.

Another sign of batching can be seen when interim queuing of work in process has been established. Work performed at one workstation is queued nearby for later transport to another workstation. This means extra work is being performed. Instead of performing the work and handing it directly to the next workstation, the work must be set down in a queue and then picked up from that queue to resume movement to the next operation. This is wasted effort adds to time delays. A better solution is needed. For example. In the farming industry it used to be common to transport product from the fields to a central factory for further processing. Modern farms will bring these operations out to the field and perform them is a rolling factory. Imagine carrots being pulled from the ground, washed, skinned, counted into bags, and placed into shipping cases ready for display in the vegetable department of the grocery store in a trailer being towed by a tractor in the field. And the wash water and carrot skins are dropped right at the field to enrich the soil for the next crop.

I do a lot of volunteering and occasionally find myself in a food kitchen helping to feed people in a shelter. The situation I see most often is one or more people building sandwiches in batches of 8 to 12 and then bringing them out to a long queue line. The long queue with intermittent delay periods is indicative of a batch process being in use. I am quick to suggest a better way. Right at the serving line we set up a continuous flow sandwich assembly workstation. Stocks of plates, bread, meat, lettuce, butter, mayonnaise, etc. are set up. Several people are assigned to keep this stock replenished. And several people are assigned to assemble sandwiches in a "push line" fashion by pulling a plate, placing bottom piece of bread, buttering the bread, dropping on meat, dropping on lettuce, spreading on mayonnaise, placing on a top piece of bread, and handing the plate to the customer. This might require one person per step or each person doing several steps, based on demand. The process can now move as fast as people can arrive to get a sandwich, no queue line. Of course, there is always someone who points out that the top and bottom breads might come from different bags of bread. Some people find this awkward because they are used to a sandwich using the adjacent pieces of bread from the same loaf. A small compromise to gain great efficiency.

Product changes

Since products are always being improved over time, there will occasionally be a change that adds, changes, or removes some parts in the parts list. This can affect the tooling being used, workstation stocking, and employee learning. Some advance planning is typically needed to determine when to make the cut-over to the new configuration. Do we use up the old parts? When will the new parts be ready? How long will it take to modify the tools, stock bins, and training? Will some product need to be reworked?

If a pull approach is being used, this is all relatively simply a matter of choosing the cut-over point and getting everything in place to support it. If a push approach were to be in use, there is added effort of finding all of the product in queues that might be affected.

Workplace Layout

Industrial Engineers will often get involved in layout of office and production spaces. The name of the game here is to minimize

An Introduction to Industrial Engineering
flowtimes for work moving about the facility while also keeping people supporting a common effort near to each other for ease of communication. It starts with defining large departmental areas and arranging them adjacent to each other. Think about the production line. Stock comes in by truck and move to the stockroom or directly to workstation stock. Product is assembled along a series of workstations and moves the product warehouse or directly to a staging area for loading into outgoing trucks. Multiple product lines might need to be fitted in. In the office area, Accounting, Engineering, and Sales departments will need space.

To do this right, good forecast data about the company is needed. What products will be built and at what quantities, how many workstations are needed, how many employees will there be and what departments will they be in.

Designing a building layout is a daunting task which usually requires many sets of eyes on it and many compromises to achieve a workable solution that does not cause inefficiency of work that will be performed there.

Workstation Layout

With workstations, it is all about reach. Stock of parts, fixtures, tools, visual aids, etc all need to be within easy reach for the assembly operator. When stock needs to be replenished during the shift, access is needed that will not interfere with work in process and maybe a signaling system will be needed so the assembly operator can indicate they need a stock person to visit soon. I like to arrange stock in a clockwise arrangement in the expected sequence of usage. Fixtures might be on a rack accessible by a short rotation of the operator's chair and tools might be suspended from above on counter-balancers for easy access and release. Bottom line is you want the workstation to support efficient assembly of product. Adapting to the assembly operators' thoughts is also important. They are the ones closets to the real work.

An Introduction to Industrial Engineering
I have enjoyed designing many workstations in my lifetime. Most have worked really well; some have needed some changes after a few days of usage. Where I find myself in awe is seeing the workstations built for certain fast-food restaurants. I am certain a small team of very experienced engineers helped to design those.

Lean

There are many books written on lean and agile work processes. Having read most of them I can attest that lean is the Industrial Engineers dream. The best practices of lean fit right in with the best practices of Industrial engineering. It's all about being efficient. I recommend reading up on lean manufacturing.

Delays

My favorite way to improve operational workflows is to collect reasons for delays. I ask each workstation operator to keep a journal about delays that affect their work. If a delay occurs, they write down how long it lasted and give it a name such as ran out of #10 screws or supervisor called a meeting. After some time, I take all of the reasons and place them in a spreadsheet for analysis. I might make a Pareto chart of them to show which have the biggest impact. Then it comes down to brainstorming solutions with the production support team that will prevent reoccurrence of the root cause for each delay. We might tackle a few each week with each change helping to prevent delays in the future and thus increasing production efficiency.

Ergonomics

Ergonomics is all about designing tools and an environment to work well with people. For me, it has always meant providing the most comfortable situation for the workers. Good lighting, fresh air, quiet environment, temperature control, and especially good seating.

Happy workers perform much better than unhappy workers. Treat everyone with respect and you get respect back.

I had a project where we were designing a new facility for new product line, and I brought up the subject of windows. The client said no windows were planned. I argued that windows will help to cheer up the workplace. And, at the end of the day when they everyone goes home after a long day of working, they can at least discuss how the weather was. The client initially stood their ground on not having windows, but they did agree to conduct a poll of their workers for their thoughts. In the end, it was windows, very big windows along with auto adjusting LED lighting for cloudy periods and nighttime. It was a cheerful and very productive facility. And the ventilation system was designed with quiet in mind which made it even nicer.

Logistics

Logistics, the process of getting things from one place to another, is a specialized part of Industrial Engineering. It is an area that needs lots of data. Where are our customers? Is it cheaper to ship overnight direct or to stage product at a warehouse near our customers? How much product should be stored? Will the product spoil? Will we need to repack it? What are the cost trades? There are a lot of factors to consider for a good logistics solution. And things are changing all of the time.

Ethics

As with any profession, ethics are important. A wise person once said it takes years to build your image of integrity and seconds to lose it. My rule has been to always take the high road on ethics. Be open, honest, and transparent. And, stay out of company politics, it will only get you in trouble.

An Introduction to Industrial Engineering

People rely on my advice, and I want it to be of the highest quality and lead to the maximum improvement for the work process. Occasionally I would find myself working alongside with an "end justifies the means" team. My response is step up my leadership and suggest approaches that fit with my high road rule. Most often, the team will agree.

For a few projects in my life, I was brought into a situation where the ethics were so bad, and my influence was so low that I would politely decline further employment with them. Yes, I am saying no to a paycheck, I refuse to earn my money in an environment that doesn't sit well with me. I just say no.

For a few years of my career, I had a side title of Producibility Engineer. This was my chance to be involved early in a product's lifecycle to influence the design such that fabricating the product would be easier. In the big picture, ease of assemble was usually not on the mind of the design engineers. I would impose a goal to assure the product was designed to use the fewest different parts and require the lowest amount of work to build it. I would come in and advise on things like molding in an alignment notch to assure parts can't be assembled wrong, using more of the same size screws to reduce parts list complexity, adding alignment pins in place of screws to assure parts fit tightly together, or adding access holes to allow testing to occur without substantial disassembly.

Robotics

Robotics have been around a long time. It has also been one of my favorite work areas. Robots can work 24/7 doing jobs repeatedly with high quality and no need for personal time off. In the early years, robots were less capable, and we had to search for tasks that they could perform. And, often we found that robot could not work as fast as a human. Over time robots have become more advanced with ability to learn a job and repeat it over and over with good speed.

It is now common to have robots working side by side with people to build products. The important part of robotics for the Industrial Engineer is allocating the right tasks and programming to perform them in the fastest way while keeping quality high.

My first career job was during the Vietnam War era where I worked for a defense contractor as a Radar Technician. These radars where part of an area defense system that would detect enemy aircraft and shoot them down using a radar guided surface to air missile. What I learned about these radars is they had power supplies, pneumatics, hydraulics, actuator valves, servo motors, and drive mechanisms, all parts common in robots. I got very good at diagnosing problems and repairing these systems. As the war ended and we were all heading for lay-offs, I used this knowledge to get a job servicing the assembly robots in the product manufacturing area.

Out in the manufacturing floor there was this one machine that installed electronic components into circuit boards. It was almost painfully loud as it moved on "kerchunking" parts at a good speed. One day, while fixing a riveting machine I noticed it used the same brand actuator valves as the component insertion machine, but it was quiet and made only a "pssst" sound when a rivet was installed. So, my curiosity got to me and I grabbed a bunch of the riveting machine's spare valves and swapped out the values in the component insertion machine. These valves had an additional component called an air cushion. The result was amazing, the big machine was now quieter, the loud kerchunk was now muted to a level about 80% quieter. Ear protection was not needed anymore and vibration when way down.

One day the machine salesperson came to visit, I think wondering why I had not been buying spare parts like other companies. He was amazed at how quiet the machine was and how fast it was running. Three weeks later I was working for his company as a field engineer installing and programming machines around the world. I loved working in the robotics field and that next five years was one of great memories and job enjoyment.

Utilization

When planning out a work process, utilization of equipment and people must be considered. My rule has always been to plan for a maximum of 80% utilization on any one piece of equipment or workstation. This gives a nice cushion for those days when things don't go right. We all have those days, and it would not be fair to plan on everyday being the same. On better days, there will be spare capacity. When things go bad, that capacity is there to support catch back so each day can end up successful. Also, keeping some spare capacity allows for time to plan on future changes such as increasing production rates. The Industrial Engineer is often called upon to determine what additional equipment and manpower will be needed to support various production rates. To do this effectively, they must know the current utilization rates and how much product is being supported.

Safety

Safety is of high concern in workplace design. No process should be unsafe. This last thing you want is for an injury to occur. When designing a workflow, you should be constantly thinking about what could go wrong, is this the safest way to proceed.

On one project I worked I noticed that workers would stand on this spigot on the side of a large vat to get up and peek at inside. There was a ladder build on the side of the vat, but it was on the other side and not easy to get to. All I could think about was what would happen if the spigot broke off? I met with the team, and we decided the best solution was to weld a step over the spigot to protect it and add a handle on the side of the vat to hold onto when jumping up to make their peek. Maybe not the most elegant solution, but a safer one.

Quality Ownership

The best way to keep quality high is to empower those doing the workers to own their quality. Creation of inspection only roles seem logical but also causes animosity between workers and does not allow the person doing an activity to learn the real quality standard and be in control. I discourage the practice of using inspectors. Doing it right the first time is always far more effective. Always include a time allowance for people to self-inspect their work. And give them the right tools to do it.

Process Problems

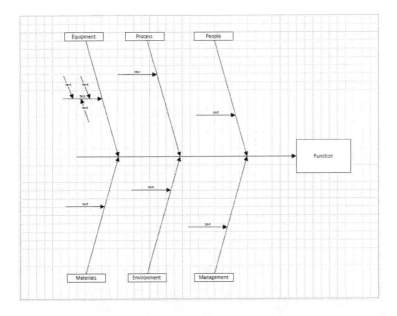

When you design a work process, right or wrong you often become its owner. I was working as a process engineer in a circuit card manufacturing company where certain circuit cards were spay coated with a clear acrylic intended to dampen the effects of long-term transportation vibration and provide water protection (parts used in high altitude military aircraft). On occasion the spray process would malfunction and leave an orange peel texture on the acrylic, making it a reject part. In this case I switched to Industrial Scientist mode. We built an Ishikawa chart of all the inputs a started a "Design of Experiments" where we varied each input to determine the point where it induced a defect. A lot was learned about mix ratios, spray speeds, and use of different solvents, but no definitive cause for this orange peel was showing up. Then the equipment operator had an idea, his theory was that orange peel occurred on rainy days (those closest to the work usually have the best inputs). Our attention was then on the air makeup system for the spray booth. It pulled fresh air directly from the outdoors (as recommended by the equipment manufacturer) and fed it into the spray booth. Wet or dry air was flowing directly into the spray based on the weather outside. Air makeup is important in spray operations and if done wrong can collapse a building due to pressure imbalance. Our solution was to install a newly invented device called an air-to-air exchanger. It took outside air into the building to make up the air we were consuming and at the same time let us pull conditioned air from inside the building for use in our spray process. By eliminating the high humidity on our intake air, orange peel was now a thing of the past.

Cost trades

Cost trades are inevitable for Industrial Engineers. There will always be questions like: Do we buy a new machine or upgrade the existing one? Do we add these new features to our current product? Or can we increase our production rate? Having performed many cost trades I can attest that most companies look for a 5-year payback on cost improvements. When it comes to increasing production rates there is often new money budgeted in advance and kicked in with the assumption that the high volume of sales will recover the investment.

My approach to cost trades is to reduce the story to a single page document with my recommendations and the cost trade numbers. This will allow the financial decision makers to know the facts and decide quickly. I store the many details supporting the cost trade in a spreadsheet that I have ready if questions about my numbers come up.

Adapting to Change

Changes are occurring all the time. Occasionally a change will affect a workflow or a role. In this case it is best discuss the change with all the people affected and mutually develop a plan with the best way to implement it. To take the "dictator" approach of just directing the change is almost always a bad approach. It says you don't care about the people, and you don't really empower them to own their jobs.

Domain Experience

For the Industrial Engineer to have deep domain experience is like a double-edged sword. If you are an expert in an industry, your solutions might be like those already in use within that industry. If you have no domain experience, your solutions might be deeper researched and new, and maybe be a better way than has ever been seen in that industry. I have been able to argue this and prove it true in several industry changes I have made over time.

When I am on a project in a new domain or familiar domain, I quickly start a deep emersion into that client's working world. I document their business language in a glossary where I can later calibrate my definitions for what each business word means.

And, when it comes to developing solutions, I do the needed deep research about the problem and call for a brainstorming session to determine a mutually agreed best solution.

Work Instructions

Industrial Engineers will often find themselves writing work instructions with step-by-step actions to perform and activity. As you write a work instruction you should also be determining the one most efficient way to perform them work.

Use Cases/User Stories

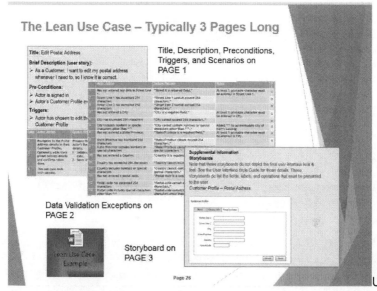

Use Cases or User Stories are a staple in the software development industry. Like a workflow, they include the trigger action (what occurred to start this process), the process steps - actor (software user) does this, system responds with this, and the exception actions. Use Cases document the one best way to perform the work.

Exception activities are those things that can occur if the actor enters data that is outside of the expected. For example, a number that is too small, too large, has letters mixed in, etc. These exceptions are very important to the quality and performance of the software product and need to be defined up front so proper coding can be developed and tested.

Another thing I like to include in my use case or user story is a visual "storyboard" of the user interface and the elements needed to support the case. This storyboard sets up expectation that these

An Introduction to Industrial Engineering
certain screen elements should be kept together in the order shown for ease of use when editing data in the workflow.

I have written 1,000s of use cases over the years and hopefully these have contributed to better software applications being built where the actions needed to use the software are logical and work efficiently.

Business Wide Efficiency

Most projects focus on a single area of improvement and most of my work has been on projects. After working projects at many clients over many years I have seen a syndrome that defies good business logic. Large and small companies seem to focus lots of attention on maximizing efficiency of the workflows for their products but seem to put little attention on the infrastructure workflows that support their product development and business sales processes. They cling to "if its not broken, don't fix it" and "we have always done it this way". The result is slow, low efficiency, and very manual infrastructure workflows eating up their profits and they find it as "normal". An example would be a company that performs monthly releases of new features instead of releasing as its completed, getting new features to market in days instead of weeks.

In these cases, I will often propose additional projects to upgrade and automate their infrastructure workflows. But it's not always easy to change a corporate culture that sees their current processes as "working just fine". Their competitors who have moved forward with automation of their support infrastructure workflows are "eating their lunch" while they accept their own current state as necessary overhead expense. A saying we use in the north is "oh well, it does create some jobs". Of course, we are being sarcastic since those jobs and their attendant cost would not be needed if the workflow were allowed to be improved.

Ego

Working for these many years I learned that my role is to be the expert on workflows. I can advise my client on ways to make improvements but should never dictate to them. They own their processes, and they have final say in the changes. In a brainstorming session I might throw in my suggestions, but I must hold back if they are thrown out when picking the best solution. My ego must stay in check.

My approach to working with clients is to come in and help define the problem in a clear statement, facilitate a brainstorming session to explore best solutions, and then lead the way forward to document and analyze the workflow and implement the team's recommendations. This approach has working well for me as I have watched many other consultants get rejected by their clients for being to "self-centered and egotistic". It comes back to the best solutions come for those closest to the workflow. Helping the team work together and develop their own best solutions works well every time.

What is more important than feeding my ego is for me to provide a positive mental attitude each day for a team approach to developing the best solutions and implementing them.

Secret Sauce

Business software applications chain together the many business workflows so they can share information with each other. However, commercial off the shelf applications are generally designed for one size fits all and contain many extra features that a particular company will never use. And most of these applications get customized to add features needed for a particular company such that later upgrades become difficult. Some companies will choose to build their own "core" business software that fits their company more perfectly and allows them to easily adapt changes over time

An Introduction to Industrial Engineering
as they become needed. Going this approach takes an investment up front but generally pays itself back in ownership of the application and efficiency to operate. In other words, the secret sauce of their business workflows remains within their corporation and can be changed to suit whenever needed.

Institute of Industrial and Systems Engineers (IISE)

As an Industrial Engineer, or even as a student of industrial engineering, you should join your professional organization. Being able to say "member of IISE" on you resume is valuable. Even more valuable is being involved in your local chapter to network and keep up with emerging trends. Or you can be a guest speaker presenting maybe a case study of a recent project. Or maybe you can be a chapter officer and help with the health of your local chapter.

My personal observation is that those people who have stayed close to their local chapter tend to show stronger leadership, are the best at their work, are willing to share their knowledge and experience, and are always in demand by their clients. Remember that life is what you make of it. If you want to be great, you need to do great things.

Conclusion

I wrote this introduction to industrial engineering for readers to determine if industrial engineering would be a good career for them. In my own life, it has worked out well for me. As I move toward retirement, I see a shortage of industrial engineers in the marketplace.

Workflows will continue to be with us for generations to come and changes in how we do business with continue to be needed. We need more serious industrial engineers out there to help facilitate workflow improvements. Maybe you will be one of these?

An Introduction to Industrial Engineering

Made in the USA
Coppell, TX
27 October 2023

23486514R00023